Guide to Eastern

ROCKS &
MINERALS

by James W. Grandy

D1565218

hancock
house

ISBN 0-88839-105-6

Copyright © 1982 James Grandy

Cataloging in Publication Data

Grandy, James
   Guide to Eastern rocks and minerals
   (Northeast color series)

   1. Rocks—Collectors and collecting—
   Northeastern States. 2. Mineralogy—
   Collectors and collecting—Northeastern
   States. I. Title. II. Series.
   QE445.N6G72   552.0974   C82-091233-6

Editor Mitchell Barnes
Typeset by Lisa Smedman in Times Roman on an AM
   Varityper Comp/Edit
Production & Layout Peter Burakoff
Printed in Canada by Friesen Printers

Hancock House Publishers Ltd.
19313 Zero Avenue, Surrey, B.C., Canada V3S 5J9
Hancock House Publishers
1431 Harrison Avenue, Blaine, WA 98230

Table of Contents

Preface

New England is a fascinating place for mineral collectors. Literally thousands of acres contain collectable material of one type or another. To cover all the areas, and all the rock and mineral types found in each, would take many huge volumes.

This book shows some of the rocks and minerals of the northeast. The majority of specimens pictured here have been collected by the author over the past twenty-two years. Some areas, such as road cuts, are gone, but most areas still contain excellent material, just sitting there waiting to be found. However, the specimens are not on top of the ground. Today it requires a lot of digging and hard work to extract them from their hiding places.

Amethyst (Quartz var.), Rt. 89 Roadcut, New London, N.H.

Geological History

The geological history of New England is very complex. The rocks of New England were, for the most part, formed during the Pre-Cambrian Era, and are among the oldest known rocks on earth. Subsequent eras and periods of geological time produced many changes. The mountains were eroded to form sediments, many of which were buried deep enough to become metamorphosed, and then were uplifted by faulting and movement of the earth to become high peaks again. Granite was formed by magma solidifying below the surface when it intruded into other rocks and was uplifted to form the White Mountains of New Hampshire. Vast areas were covered with water, and upon subsequent dropping and uplifting became the limestones and marble on the surface today. During the Carboniferous Period, coal was formed in Rhode Island. The Triassic-Jurassic Period brought the sedimentation of the valley running through the central part of Massachusetts and Connecticut. A good deal of volcanic activity took place during this time, and is in evidence today in the basalt and diabase dikes and sills that now stand as abrupt hills as a result of subsequent faulting throughout this area. Then about 10,000 years ago, the area was covered with a thousand feet or more of ice and snow in the Glacial Period. As the glaciers moved slowly southward they carried any loose material with them and redistributed it upon the land, filling in valleys and leaving hills of glacial till and many huge boulders, called glacial-erratics, sitting on top of the ground.

Weathering, stream and wind erosion, wave action along the shore line, and even a slight earth tremor in Connecticut in 1980 continue to have an effect on the ever-changing surface of New England.

Metamorphic Rocks Showing Folding, Rt. 8, Reynolds Bridge, Watertown, Conn.

5

Collecting and the Collector

The first rock and mineral collector must have been a cave dweller who saw a pretty stone and picked it up. Ever since then, rocks and minerals have been sought after for many reasons. But only recently has it been possible for amateurs to learn the techniques and obtain the equipment necessary to cut and polish or facet their own stones.

This cutting and polishing of stones, or lapidary as it is officially called, is only a minor part of rock and mineral collecting in the New England area. In contrast to collectors in the western states, where lapidary is a growing hobby all on its own, the New England collectors consider lapidary a sideline.

Every collector tends to specialize, consciously or not, because of a preference for a certain mineral species or location. Some people collect only rocks, and others only minerals; some collect only cutting material (rocks or minerals), while many collect only crystallized mineral specimens. Many collections are confined to rocks and minerals of a certain size. *Museum specimens* are generally the largest, weighing up to a hundred pounds or more. However, this classification does not always refer to quality, and most specimens of this size would not meet museum standards for display. *Cabinet specimens* or hand specimens range in size from 2″ to 10″. *Miniatures* are no bigger than 2″ in any direction, while *thumbnails* must fit into a 1″ cube. Other enthusiasts collect only microscopic crystals and create their own micromounts. Micromounts

Dolomite Slab, Colebrook, Vermont.

Jasper-Agate (Quartz var.), Hamden, Conn.

are specimens that are permanently mounted and require magnification and illumination for proper viewing and study. The typical micromount box is 1″ x 1″ x 7/8″.

Some collectors enjoy cutting and polishing their specimens. Many of the rocks such as dolomite and serpentine, as well as the more common quartz family and feldspar groups, qualify as cutting material, suitable for tumbling and making cabochons. A cabochon in its simplest form has one flat and one curved surface. The term originated from the Latin word *caput*, a head. Maine and Connecticut are famous for their pegmatites (see How to Identify a Rock), which yield gem quality tourmaline and many lesser known minerals for the facetor.

Serpentine (Slab), Rock River, S. Newfane, Vermont.

Rhodonite, Polished Heart Cabochon.

7

Flint (Quartz var.), Hamden, Conn.

Fluorapatite, Palermo Mine, N. Groton, N.H.

Where Are the Specimens?

The best place to look for specimens is in old mines or quarries that have piles of waste material. Don't go into old mine tunnels or climb quarry walls, as these areas can be very dangerous. New road cuts or any area under construction might also yield good material.

Trading is a good way to obtain specimens. Many mineral clubs have swaps and shows. Or you can use the "silver pick" method and buy your specimens from a dealer.

To make it easier to know what you are looking for and how to identify your specimens, you must buy a good rock and mineral textbook and you must do your homework. Many states and regional areas also have books and pamphlets about specific locations where you may collect. But the best advice of all is to join a mineral club, where you'll find many people to help you. (See Appendix A.)

Elbaite (Tourmaline Group), Plumbago Gem Mine, Newry, Maine.

Rhodonite, Betts Manganese Mine, Plainfield, Mass. Massachusetts State Gem.

Almandine (Garnet Group), Greens Farm, Roxbury, Conn. Connecticut State Mineral.

Good Manners

There is very little, if any, public land in New England where you can just go and collect. Even the White Mountains National Forest in New Hampshire has an "advance permit required" system. Before going on private land you must ask permission or suffer the anger of the landowner. Plan ahead! Check out the area you wish to visit, and if the owner's answer is no, or the area is posted, find another locality. More areas are closed because of lack of respect for the land and its owner than for any other reason.

When you do enter an area, please show the proper respect. Use common sense. Make sure all gates are closed. Don't litter, don't throw rocks, and don't leave large gaping holes—fill them in! Treat the land as though it were your own.

We are only here on earth for a very short period of time, geologically speaking. While we are here we should serve our stewardship well and remember to leave the land better than we found it.

Silicified Wood (Quartz Var.). Lake Zoar. Newtown, Conn.

Amethystine Quartz, Canton, Conn.

Equipment; Gloves, Crack Hammer, Chisels, Hard Hat & Safety Glasses, Sledge (Maul).

Equipment

The amount and type of equipment needed will depend on the type of collecting you intend to do. A geologist's pick with belt carrier, a sledge hammer, and a magnifying glass are standard for all. If you're going to be a "dump digger," then you'll need a shovel and a ¼" screen. If you want to be a "hard-rock miner," then you'll need a variety of chisels and a two-to-four-pound crack hammer. Safety equipment includes a hard hat, safety glasses, and steel-toed boots. Never wear sneakers or open-toed sandals into a collecting area. A knapsack to carry your equipment and a cloth or canvas bag to carry your specimens out are useful. Don't forget to carry some newspaper to wrap the fragile crystal specimens, and an egg carton for small pieces. You can always add more equipment as you go along.

Equipment; Screen, Shovel, Pick & Case, Magnifying Glass.

Definitions

Before discussing rocks and minerals, let us start with a couple of definitions. Some examples of terminology are also in order. "Naturally occurring" means that specimens are "as found in nature," not man-made. Rocks and minerals are made from approximately 80 of the more than 100 elements, the remainder being inert gases, short-lived atomic elements, or man-made ones. "Organic" rocks consist of once-living material; "inorganic" means that they were never living substances (although in some, like silicified wood, the original form has been replaced molecule by molecule with quartz).

What Is a Rock?

A rock is a naturally occurring solid that forms a major land mass and is made up of one or more minerals. The specimen you hold in your hand is a *piece* of a rock.

Granite is a good example. It always contains quartz, feldspar, and biotite mica. In addition, several other minerals, such as muscovite mica, hornblende, magnetite, and tourmaline are sometimes found in this rock type.

White Granite and Pink Granite, New Hampshire.

What Is a Mineral?

A mineral is a naturally occurring inorganic substance. It is made up of one or more elements in certain amounts. Each mineral has a definite crystal structure. Approximately 3,000 minerals are known at the present time.

11

Smoky Quartz and Microcline Feldspar, Conway, N.H.

Smoky Quartz and Microcline Feldspar, Conway, N.H.

Watermelon Tourmaline (Elbaite), White Rocks Quarry, Middletown, Conn.

Copper, for instance, is a single-element mineral, denoted by the chemical shorthand symbol Cu. The mineral quartz is composed of two elements, silicon (Si) and oxygen (O), in a ratio of one part silicon to two of oxygen—SiO_2. Some minerals, like tourmaline, have as many as twelve elements in their composition, and some have more.

What Is a Crystal?

Crystals of minerals are formed when molten material, liquids, or vapors cool. If there is enough room, beautiful crystal faces are formed. These are the external plane surfaces that reflect the internal arrangement of the atoms. These solids then have a specific set of faces, edges, and corners.

Spodumene Crystal, Chandler Mine, Raymond, N.H.

The rate of cooling and the time a mineral has to crystallize determine the size. Large crystals often have many distortions, and it is not until you get down to microsize that you approach true perfection. Small crystals are sharper and clearer, and hence better for observation and study. It is this perfection and beauty in the smaller samples, plus the fact that many minerals only occur in microsize crystals, that has led to the popularity of collecting micromounts.

Often, when one shows non-collector friends a quartz crystal, they will exclaim, "Oh, that's beautiful, how did you make it?" Sometimes they just can't believe that the crystals are natural.

Magnetite Crystal, Madison, Conn.

Beryl, Pelton Quarry, Portland, Conn.

Schorl (Tourmaline Group), Bethel Pegmatite, Bethel, Conn.

Identification

Well, now that you have spent some happy hours in the field collecting specimens, what have you found? A professional's laboratory has many aids to identification, such as chemical analysis, X-ray diffraction, and use of a polarizing microscope, but these are not usually available to the amateur. However, you can probably succeed in identifying most specimens.

First, make sure you record the location that was visited; knowing the mineral's environment will make identification easier. Usually the first question asked is, "Where did you find it?"

It is not within the scope of this book to give you all the data necessary for identification, but I hope to whet your appetite so that you will do some further studying.

It is also important to buy and use a good mineral book and carefully study the external features of your specimen.

How to Identify a Crystal

Minerals are divided into six crystal systems, depending on the number of the axes, their angles, and their length in relation to one another. Crystallography is a very difficult subject, and one that requires careful study. The crystals must be properly oriented if the angles and faces are to be correctly identified.

The systems are:

1) THE CUBIC OR ISOMETRIC SYSTEM, which has three axes of equal length, all at right angles to one another. Examples are: galena, fluorite, and pyrite.

Pyrite, Iron Mine,
Roxbury, Conn.

2) THE TETRAGONAL SYSTEM also has three axes at right angles to one another. Two axes are of equal length and the third, the vertical axis, is longer or shorter. Examples are: zircon, autunite, rutile, and chalcopyrite.

Uraninite (Black), Montmorillonite (Pink), and Autunite (Yellow-Green), Ruggles Mine, Grafton, N.H.

3) THE ORTHORHOMBIC SYSTEM maintains the three axes all at right angles to one another, but they are of unequal lengths. Examples are: barite, staurolite, and topaz.

4) THE MONOCLINIC SYSTEM has three axes of unequal length, two at right angles, with the third inclined to the vertical. Examples are: mica, epidote, and malachite.

Barite Crystals, Jinny Hill Mine, Cheshire, Conn.

Muscovite Mica, Globe Mine, Springfield, N.H.

5) THE TRICLINIC SYSTEM has three axes of unequal length, all inclined to one another so that there are no right angles. Examples are: kyanite, rhodonite, and plagioclase feldspars.

6) THE HEXAGONAL SYSTEM has four axes. Three are of equal length at 120° angles in a horizontal plane, while the fourth axis is at right angles to them and is either longer or shorter. Examples are: quartz, beryl, and tourmaline.

Smoky Quartz, Morris Dam, East Morris, Conn.

How to Identify a Mineral

A large number of minerals can be identified by their external physical features with or without an external crystal shape. These require only careful study of the specimen and relatively simple tests.

Color—Minerals come in every color and shape imaginable. Some

Heterosite, Palermo Mine #1, N. Groton, N.H.

minerals have a very distinctive color, and some have many colors. Color can be very deceiving and should never be used as the only means of identification.

Luster—Now is your specimen shiny or dull, or does it look like a metal? The surface of your specimen gives another clue to its identity. One that resembles metal is called metallic. If it is extremely brilliant like a diamond it is called adamantine, and if glassy like quartz it is vitreous. If it absorbs all the light it might be termed earthy or dull, and if fibrous in nature it would be called silky. There are about a dozen different lusters.

Elbaite (Tourmaline Group), Strickland Quarry, Portland, Conn.

Jasper (Quartz var.), Parrot Jasper Mine, Colchester, Vermont.

17

Schorl (Tourmaline Group), Mt. Tom, Moodus, Conn.

Almandine (Garnet Group), Bennett Quarry Buckfield, Mass.

Hardness—This is a scratch test. It was devised by a German named Mohs in 1822. Although not completely accurate, it gives you an indication by comparison of the specimen's hardness. The Mohs scale is: **(1)** Talc, **(2)** Gypsum, **(3)** Calcite, **(4)** Fluorite, **(5)** Apatite, **(6)** Orthoclase Feldspar, **(7)** Quartz, **(8)** Topaz, **(9)** Corundum, **(10)** Diamond. If the specimen you have will scratch calcite but not fluorite, for instance, then it is said to have a hardness of 3½. Some minerals have a different hardness when scratched in a different direction, so try more than one spot. Remember not to scratch a crystal face, as you might ruin the specimen. In the field you can use your fingernail, which has a hardness of about 2½, or a knife blade, which has a hardness of 5½.

Streak—A piece of unglazed porcelain has a hardness of about 7. Any mineral softer than this can be scratched on the porcelain to obtain a mark or streak, which is the true color of the powdered mineral. This test is usually used for the metals.

Cleavage—Certain minerals break along flat planes that are in relation to their molecular structure. This is called cleavage. Strike a broken crystal or massive specimen lightly with a hammer and observe the pieces. The best-known example is mica, with its basal cleavage. Galena will always break into cubes and calcite into rhombohedrons. Many minerals have one or more cleavages, and this is an important test.

Fracture—If your specimen shows no sign of a cleavage when broken, you can still identify it by its fracture. A metal with jagged edges is said to have a hackly fracture. Quartz has a curving, shell-like fracture called conchoidal. Clay is said to have an earthy fracture.

Specific Gravity—The specific gravity is the weight of the mineral in relation to the weight of an equal volume of water. The size of the specimen is not important, but it must be of one mineral only, as impurities will cause incorrect readings. To obtain the specific gravity you need a balance scale. Weigh the specimen in air on a string or wire, then weigh the same specimen in water. Subtract the weight in water from the weight in air to determine the amount of weight lost. Divide the weight in air by the loss of weight, and this figure will be the specific gravity.

Other Tests—Many other tests for such properties as magnetism, fluorescence, radioactivity, and electrical conductivity can be made. Most mineral textbooks contain the specifics on each of the more common minerals.

However, the very best way to identify specimens, especially microcrystals, is by familiarity. You recognize good friends by their size, structure, color of hair, skin, and eyes, by their companions, and by the car or place they are in. Well, you can do this with many different minerals once you have made their acquaintance and have spent some time with them. This is by no means a scientific method, or even a certain way of ensuring identification, but after a little practice you'll be surprised at your own accuracy. To do this you must be dedicated and constantly study your specimens, your friends' collections, museum collections, dealer's displays, and other sources you have access to. Start by learning the common specimens and build up gradually to the rarer ones, perhaps specializing in one locality or chemical group at a time.

Beryl, Pelton Quarry, Portland, Conn.

Chert (Quartz var.), Hamden, Conn.

Iron Stained Milky Quartz Crystals, Diamond Ledge, W. Stafford Springs, Conn.

Childrenite, Black Mountain, Rumford, Maine.

How to Identify a Rock

Rocks are grouped into three major categories depending upon their mode of origin. In New England we are fortunate to have examples of all three. As mentioned in the preface, it would be impossible to describe all the types of formations and the minerals found in them, so I have chosen some of the most important rock types in which good mineral specimens may be found. Before collecting in a given area it is a good idea to learn as much about its geological history as possible.

Igneous

This word comes from the Greek word meaning "fire-formed." Igneous rocks are formed from molten material called magma. The rate of cooling determines the size of the mineral grains formed. Common examples are granite, basalt, diabase, and pegmatite.

Pegmatite is an intrusive igneous rock. Because it is formed below the surface of the earth from molten material and hot gases and cooled very slowly, it can contain very large mineral crystals. The word

Igneous Rocks, Diabase (Traprock) Cliffs, West Rock Ridge, Woodbridge, Conn.

Arfvedsonite, Hurricane Mountain, Conway, N.H.

Morganite (Beryl var.), Gillette Quarry, Haddam Neck, Conn.

"pegmatite" refers to the gross composition of the crystalline formation and the manner in which it was formed. Although other pegmatites are known to occur, the name usually refers to granite pegmatites. These are composed chiefly of quartz, mica, and feldspar but can also contain many rare minerals.

New England is famous for its pegmatites, found as veins or dikes in other rock types. Chesterfield, Massachusetts, has a notable lithium pegmatite, and Connecticut has many in the Middletown-Portland area and some in the western part of the state as well. New Hampshire has the famous Ruggles Mine and one of my favorite collecting areas for rare phosphate minerals, the Palermo Mine in North Groton, New Hampshire. Maine has many fine, well-known pegmatites. The 1972-73 find of several large pockets of gem-quality tourmaline in the old Dunton Quarry, in the newly mined area then named the Plumbago Gem Mine, Newry, Maine, pales all other finds by comparison.

Autunite, Cyrtolite, and Uranium Secondaries, Ruggles Mine, Grafton, N.H.

21

Elbaite (Tourmaline Group), Black Mountain, Rumford, Maine.

Golden Beryl, Larry Mine, Grafton, N.H.

A few of the minerals found in pegmatite are: beryl, tourmaline (elbaite and schorl), lepidolite, fluorite, apatite, childrenite, topaz, and spodumene.

Basalt and Diabase are similar in their dark color and in mineral composition, and both are referred to as "trap rock" in New England. Basalt is an extrusive rock, having formed above the surface of the earth from lava flows. Diabase is an intrusive rock that formed just below the surface, giving it a coarser texture.

Each state in New England has representative formations of one or both types. The best-known sites for collectors are the two old lava flows in the Perry, Maine, area, where the gas trapped in the fast-cooling basalt left almond-shaped holes, which later filled with quartz. Weathering and the beating of the ocean waves have broken up the

Calcite, Rt. 91 Roadcut, Bellows Falls, Vermont.

Natrolite & Analcime, Trap Quarry, Cheshire, Conn.

Datolite on Prehnite, Roncari Quarry, East Granby, Conn.

rock, leaving the quartz nodules lying on the beach. Massachusetts's two most popular areas are the Bayer-Mingolla Quarry in Ashland and the Blueberry Mountain Quarry in Woburn. In Connecticut, where diabase predominates, the popular spots are the Roncari Quarry in East Granby, the Reeds Gap Quarry on the Wallingford-Durham town line, and the Cheshire Trap Quarry, Cheshire. However, these quarries at present are usually closed to collectors.

The zeolites are a group of minerals found in these rock types. Some zeolites are: analcime, natrolite, stilbite, and chabazite. Other minerals found are datolite, apophyllite, pyrite, fluorite, and quartz.

Sedimentary

Sedimentary rocks are formed by the deposition and consolidation of loose material and the subsequent application of pressure with a little heat and a cementing agent. The cementing agent of the great Triassic Valley, which stretches from Long Island Sound in New Haven, Connecticut, through Massachusetts to the Vermont border, was iron oxide, and this gives the formation a distinctive red color. Sedimentary rocks usually appear as beds or layers. Common examples are arkose, sandstone, conglomerate, limestone, and shale.

Tremolite and Pyrite, Canaan, Conn.

Pyrite in Shale, Rt. 89 Roadcut, Montpelier, Vermont.

Barite on Sandstone, Jinny Hill Mine, Cheshire, Conn.

Sandstone is made up of small grains of a uniform size formed from pre-existing eroded rocks and held rather loosely together. This is the dominant rock of the Triassic Valley. The largest number of dinosaur tracks in the world have been uncovered in the sandstone at Rocky Hill, Connecticut. Some of the minerals found are: calcite, barite, native copper, malachite, and quartz.

Limestone usually forms from an accumulation of dead organisms at the bottom of a body of water. It is made up almost completely of calcite, which originally came from the land and was then extracted from the water by the organisms. When they in turn died and sank to the bottom, the natural forces of sedimentation took over, and pressure compacted them into rock. If the crustal movements of the earth pushed them up, they would remain limestone; however, if they sank downwards to any great depth, they would be metamorphosed into marble.

Limestone has been mined in every New England state. Some of the mines, such as the Conklin Quarries in northwestern Connecticut and those in Rhode Island, are still active.

Common minerals found in limestone are: calcite, dolomite, galena, sphalerite, fluorite, and goethite.

Temolite, Canaan, Conn.

Goethite, Lakeville, Salisbury, Conn.   Calcite, Rt. 7 Roadcut, Brookfield, Conn.

Metamorphic

This word means "changed-form." Both igneous and sedimentary rocks may be transformed by heat and pressure into this third type of rock. The deep-seated rocks become very hot and actually plastic in nature. Because of the tremendous heat and pressure, the mineral grains have a tendency to line up in layers and in some instances even re-crystallize. The layers often become bent and folded. Common examples are: marble, gneiss, schist, quartzite, and slate.

Andalusite var., Chiastolite, Sterling, Mass.   Epidote, Rt.9 Roadcut, Haddam, Conn.

25

Cordierite Crystal, Soapstone Quarry, Richmond, N.H.

Chabazite, Sandy Hook-Newtown Roadcut, Conn.

Gneiss (pronounced nice) can have several origins. The most common in New England is the granite gneiss, which is metamorphosed granite. This rock is rich in feldspar, with the biotite mica in layers of varying widths, creating a black and white banded appearance. Minerals found in gneiss include: ilmenite, kyanite, and cordierite.

Mica Schist is highly metamorphosed rock formed from shale rich in mica or from phyllite. This type of rock is often called the basement rock of the mountains. It usually has a wavy structure and varies in color from silvery gray in the muscovite type to black in the biotite type. This type of mica schist has re-crystallized into small flakes, which can

Staurolite, Windham, Maine.

26

easily be seen with the naked eye. The mica and quartz form layers similar to gneiss, with the mica layers much finer in the schist. Mica schist is common in all the New England states, and indicates to the geologist where the mountains once stood.

Minerals found here are: chlorite, pyrite, graphite, calcite, staurolite, garnet, zircon, apatite, ilmenite, and schorl tourmaline.

Actinolite, Carlton Mine, Chester, Vermont.

Pyrite on Phyllite with Calcite, Woodbridge, Conn.

Gold and Gold Panning

Gold has been found in placer deposits in every state in New England. Although not as plentiful as in the west, it still draws a lot of attention when it is mentioned. It would be very difficult to earn a living panning gold in this area. The report of the *Vermont State Geologist* in 1919-20 refers the reader to *The Geology of Vermont,* published in 1861, which says in part, "We give it as our opinion that not one in ten who have engaged in gold washing in that town (Plymouth) has realized as much from it as he would have done by working on a farm at ordinary wages." However, as a hobby panning is lots of fun. Finding those gold colors in the bottom of the pan is always exciting.

Native Gold Nugget, Panned in 1980, Plymouth, Vermont.

27

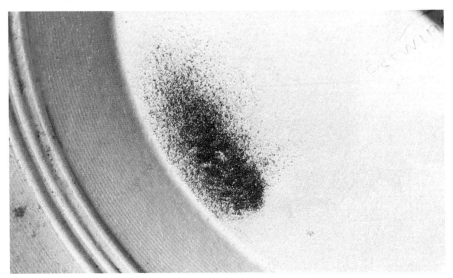
Gold Pan with Concentrate, Plymouth, Vermont area.

Mining in New England, Past and Present

Following the arrival of the *Mayflower* on the shore of Massachusetts in 1620, more and more colonists came to the new world to seek their fortunes. English noblemen, unable to leave home, also sent emissaries to search for valuable ore deposits. Upon finding and sending a recognized or unknown ore back to England by ship, the searchers of yesterday and their patrons were probably as excited as the astronauts of today were when they returned with their first payload of rocks from the moon.

Unofficially, the first rock to be used was probably granite. All the New England states that border on the Atlantic Ocean have had granite quarries along the shore, and although Vermont does not have a coastline it boasts of the world's largest granite quarry in Barre. Many of these quarries are now merely overgrown holes in the ground, but a few, such as the one in Barre, still produce stone for buildings and monuments. However, New Hampshire is known as the Granite State.

In 1709 the first chartered English mining company in America was established as the Simsbury Copper Mines in Connecticut. This area later became part of Granby and, with a final sub-division, now is in the town of East Granby. During the Revolutionary War the mine was used as the first Connecticut colonial prison, and it later became Connecticut's first state prison. To this day it is better known as the "Old Newgate Prison." The mine produced a large quantity of native copper and ore, and was worked for many years by the prisoners during and after the Revolution. The historic ruins are still owned by the State of Connecticut and can be viewed as a tourist attraction.

The pegmatites became popular in New England in 1803 when mica was first produced commercially at the Ruggles mine in Grafton, New Hampshire. This mine is right on the top of the Isinglass Mountain and is also open to tourists. A maintained dirt road will take you to the top, and for a small fee you may walk around in the open mine and dig in the dumps for some of the 150 minerals found there.

Mica was in great demand in England for lamp chimneys and stove windows. Sam Ruggles knew this, and when he found the mica on the top of the mountain he decided to keep his mining work a secret. For many years the mica was hauled to Portsmouth for shipment to England. It was hidden under farm produce and taken by ox team, or transported by horse and buggy or sleigh in the dead of night. When many new uses for mica were discovered, General Electric leased the mine and worked it for several years. Then the Bon Ami Company leased the mine for feldspar.

During these operations beryl was one of the chief accessory minerals, and it was saved and sold to the government. Beryl was mined in four of the New England states, but New Hampshire was the leader, listing eighteen towns in which beryl was commercially mined. A recent increase in the government's price for beryl has reawakened an interest in its production, and some of the old pegmatites are being looked at again.

Another new source of interest for mining is uranium. Following the

Siderite Crystals, Iron Mine, Roxbury, Conn.

29

Wolframite, Old Mine Park, Trumbull, Conn.

big search of the late forties, the demand died down. But now there seems to be renewed interest in the granites and pegmatites of New Hampshire for this ore.

Garnet was mined in New England in several areas. Connecticut, Massachusetts, and New Hampshire all have old mines. The discovery of a large garnet deposit in Maine recently has created some excitement for mining potential there.

Many buildings, walls, and monuments in Connecticut and in New York City were built in the early 1900s of "brown stone." This was sandstone from the quarries along the Connecticut River in Portland, Connecticut.

Most of the New England states have old iron mines and also limestone quarries necessary to help smelt the ore. The Roxbury Iron Mine in Connecticut is now owned by the Roxbury Land Trust and will be held in perpetuity. Collecting there is allowed with advance permission from the land trust.

Vermont is the leader of all the New England states in the production of marble, and it has been nicknamed "The Marble State." The quarries in West Rutland have always been known as "the largest marble quarries in the world." The Danby Marble Company, Danby, Vermont, supplied the stone for the Jefferson Memorial in Washington, D.C., and I'm sure many other famous buildings came from the New England hills.

In the early 1900s Vermont was also noted for its slate production. In 1920, the Vermont Milling and Products Corporation was one of the first companies to grind up their slate, screen it, and bind it with asphalt upon a fiber material. The resulting slabs were then cut to proper size, and our first slate-asphalt shingles were born.

The Palermo Mine in North Groton, New Hampshire, has been worked over the years for mica, feldspar, beryl, and more recently for the rare phosphate minerals it contains. These minerals are not of economic importance, but are of great interest to the thumbnail and micromount collector. Serious collectors from Europe have made "field trips" here to collect these unique specimens. Collecting is permitted for a small fee.

Most of the mines and quarries in New England are closed now: some were worked out, some ran into economic difficulty, and some produced materials that are no longer in demand. Mother Nature has taken over the old roads and dumps. Trees and natural litter hide the scars on the hillsides, making the areas difficult for all but the hardy, alert collector to find. But specimens are there, waiting to be found and brought out into the light for all to enjoy their beauty.

Autunite "Eye"
Hale Quarry,
Portland, Conn.

Serpentine, variety Chrysotile Asbestos, Johnston, Rhode Island.

Appendix A

Rock and Mineral Clubs in New England

CONNECTICUT

City: Bridgeport
Name: Bridgeport Mineralogical Society
Contact: Ted Bresky, 5 Austin Dr., Easton, CT 06612

City: Bristol
Name: Bristol Gem and Mineral Club, Inc.
Contact: Dr. William E. Furniss, Ichobod Lane, Burlington, CT 06013

City: Danbury
Name: Danbury Mineralogical Society, Inc.
Contact: Mike DeLuca, 448 Limestone Rd., Ridgefield, CT 06877

City: East Hartford
Name: Nutmeg Gemcrafters
Contact: Larry Cross, 61 Alton St., Manchester, CT 06040

City: Meriden
Name: Lapidary and Mineral Society of Central Connecticut
Contact: Marcianne MacDonald, 57 East Summer St., Plantsville, CT 06479

City: Middletown
Name: Middlesex County Mineral Club, Inc.
Contact: John C. Williams, RFD 1, Box 131D, Moodus, CT 06469

City: New Britain (Central Conn. State College)
Name: Connecticut Fossil Club
Contact: Martin H. Francis, 56 Water St., S. Glastonbury, CT 06073

City: New Haven
Name: New Haven Mineral Club, Inc.
Contact: Club Address, 524 Brooksvale Ave., Hamden, CT 06518

City: New London
Name: Thames Valley Rockhounds
Contact: Verna Skinner, 11 Shore Rd., Waterford, CT 06385

City: Stamford
Name: Stamford Mineralogical Society, Inc.
Contact: Club Address, P.O. Box 2073, Stamford, CT 06906

City: Westport
Name: The Nature Center for Environmental Activities Mineral Group
Contact: The Center, 10 Woodside Lane, P.O. Box 165, Westport, CT 06880

Connecticut Council of Mineral, Lapidary & Fossil Clubs
Chairman: Howard Van Iderstine, 2 Tulip Lane, Huntington, CT 06484

MASSACHUSETTS

City: Auburn
Name: New England Prospectors
Contact: Harold Herard, 2 Betty St., Auburn, MA 01501

City: Braintree
Name: Southeastern Mass. Mineral Club, Inc.
Contact: John Anderson, Jr., 386 Whiting Ave., Dedham, MA 02025

City: Brewster
Name: Cape Cod Gem and Mineral Club
Contact: John Cronan, Box 672, N. Eastham, MA 02651

City: Framingham
Name: Framingham Gem and Mineral Club
Contact: Edward Boyd, 14 Fenmore Ave., Wellesley, MA 02181

City: Greenfield
Name: Franklin County Mineral Club of Mass.
Contact: John Oski, 9 Oak Hill Rd., Greenfield, MA 01301

City: Lynn
Name: Lynn Mineral Club
Contact: Joseph Balsama, 23 Sherwood Rd., Swampscott, MA 01907

City: Lynnfield
Name: North Shore Rock & Mineral Club of Mass., Inc.
Contact: Fred Bass, 556 Shirley St., Winthrop, MA 02152

City: North Adams
Name: Northern Berkshire Mineral Club
Contact: Robert Dion, 188 State St., N. Adams, MA 01247

City: Pittsfield
Name: Museum Greylock Mineral Club
Contact: Edna Lerer, P.O. Box 157, Maynard, MA 01754

City: Springfield
Name: Connecticut Valley Mineral Club
Contact: Stuart Benson, Kibbe Dr., Somers, CT

City: Westford
Name: Nashoba Valley Mineralogical Society
Contact: Edna Lerer, P.O. Box 157, Maynard, MA 01754

City: Westminster
Name: Westminster Mineral Club
Contact: Steven Higley, 44 Sand St., Gardener, MA 01440

City: Worcester
Name: Worcester Mineral Club, Inc.
Contact: Donald Wiles, Box 99, Glendale Station, MA 01606

Association of Massachusetts Mineral Clubs
President: Don Wiles (Worchester Mineral Club)

VERMONT

City: Brattleboro
Name: Mineralogical Society of Brattleboro
Contact: Earl R. Melendy, Museum Terrace, S. Londonderry,   VT 05155
City: Burlington
Name: Burlington Gem and Mineral Club
Contact: Ethel Schuele, 33 Clover St., S. Burlington, VT 05401
City: Rutland
Name: Rutland Rock and Mineral Club
Contact: Marlene Dawson, 23 School St., Wallingford, VT 05773
City: Springfield
Name: Springfield Mineralogical Society
Contact: Elva (Nelson) Longe, 5 Leonard Ave., Springfield, VT 05156

RHODE ISLAND

City: Providence
Name: The Rhode Island Mineral Hunters
Contact: Ralph L. Carr, 25 Farnum Rd., Warwick, RI 02888

MAINE

City: Calais
Name: St. Croix International Gem and Mineral Club
Contact: Club Address, P.O. Box 266, Calais, ME 04619
City: Farmington
Name: Sandy River Mineral Club
Contact: Gary Hutchinson, Carthage, ME
City: Lewiston
Name: Lincoln Co. Gem and Mineral Society
Contact: Lane Soltesz, 21 Williams Ave., Topsam, ME 04086
City: Portland
Name: Coastal Maine Mineral Club
Contact: George Bonney, RFD #1, Box 225, Norway, ME 04268
City: Portland
Name: Maine Mineralogical and Geological Society, Inc.
Contact: Robert Phillips, Sr., Cascade Rd., Old Orchard Beach, ME 04064
City: Rumford
Name: Oxford County Gem and Mineral Society
Contact: Club Address, P.O. Box 353, Rumford, ME 04276
City: Waterville
Name: Water Oak Gem and Mineral Society
Contact: Club Address, P.O. Box 47, Waterville, ME 04901
Maine Federation of Mineral Clubs
Bob Phillips, Cascade Rd., Old Orchard Beach, ME 04064

NEW HAMPSHIRE

City: Concord
Name: Capital Mineral Club
Contact: Joanne Caswell, P.O. Box 411, Concord, NH 03301

City: Conway
Name: Saco Valley Gem and Mineral Club
Contact: Brownlow Thompson, Box 263, Conway, NH 03818

City: Keene
Name: Keene Mineral Club
Contact: Robert L. Braden, 33 Hilltop Dr., Keene, NH 03431

City: Laconia
Name: Lakes Region Mineral Society
Contact: Gladys Burrows, Holderness Rd., Center Sandwich, NH 03227

City: Nashua
Name: Nashua Mineral Society
Contact: Marlene York, 5 Roberts Rd., Stow, MA

City: Rochester
Name: Southeastern N.H. Mineral Club
Contact: William Higgins, 42 Court St., Exeter, NH 03833

Appendix B

Physical Properties of Common New England Minerals

	CHEMICAL FORMULA	CRYSTAL SYSTEM	COLOR
Almandine (Garnet)	$Fe_3^{+2}Al_2(SiO_4)_3$	Cubic	Dark red
Autunite	$Ca(UO_2)_2(PO_4)_2 \cdot 10\text{-}12H_2O$	Tetragonal	Yellow
Barite	$BaSO_4$	Orthorhombic	Colorless to white
Beryl	$Be_3Al_2Si_6O_{18}$	Hexagonal	Varied
Brazilianite	$NaAl_3(PO_4)_2(OH)_4$	Monoclinic	Yellow-green
Calcite	$CaCO_3$	Hexagonal (Rhombic)	Varied
Childrinite	$Fe^{+2}Al(PO_4)(OH)_2 \cdot H_2O$	Monoclinic	Tan to brown
Copper	Cu	Cubic	Copper-red
Datolite	$CaBSiO_4(OH)$	Monoclinic	Pale green
Elbaite (Tourmaline)	$Na(Li,Al)_3Al_6(BO_3)_3Si_6O_{18}(OH)_4$	Hexagonal (Rhombic)	Pink, green
Epidote	$Ca_2(Al,Fe^{+3})_3(SiO_4)_3(OH)$	Monoclinic	Various, green
Galena	PbS	Cubic	Gray
Gold	Au	Cubic	Yellow, gold
Heterosite	$Fe^{+3}PO_4$	Orthorhombic	Purple
Kyanite	Al_2SiO_5	Triclinic	Blue
Magnetite	$Fe^{+2} Fe_2^{+3}O_4$	Cubic	Black
Muscovite (Mica)	$KAl_2(Si_3Al)O_{10}(OH)_2$	Monoclinic	Silvery white
Pollucite	$(Cs,Na)_2Al_2Si_4O_{12} \cdot H_2O$	Cubic	Colorless
Pyrite	FeS_2	Cubic	Brass yellow
Quartz	SiO_2	Hexagonal (Rhombic)	Varied
Rhodonite	$(Mn^{+2},Fe^{+2},Mg,Ca)SiO_3$	Triclinic	Pink

CLEAVAGE	SPECIFIC GRAVITY	LUSTER	HARDNESS	FAMILIARITY
None	4.1	Vitreous	7	Color, crystal form
Basal	3.1	Pearly	2-2.5	Color, green fluorescence
Basal Prismatic	4.5	Vitreous	2.5-3.5	Very heavy for white mineral
None	2.6	Vitreous	7.5-8	Crystal form, associations
Perfect	2.9	Vitreous	3.5-4	Many crystal faces, location
Rhombohedral	2.7	Vitreous to Pearly	3	Perfect rhombohedral cleavage
None	3.2	Vitreous	5	Crystal form, associations
None	8.9	Metallic	2.5-3	Color, structure
None	2.8	Brilliant to Vitreous	5-5.5	Luster, location
None	3.0	Vitreous	7-7.5	Color, crystal form
Basal	3.4	Vitreous	6-7	Color, striated faces
Cubic	7.5	Metallic	7.5	Specific gravity, cubic crystal, cleavage
None	19.2	Metallic	2.5-3	Color in pan
Perfect	3.4	Resinous	5.5-6	Color
Pinacoidal	3.6	Vitreous	5-7	Color, crystals
None	5.1	Metallic	6	Octohedral crystal shape
Basal	2.8	Pearly	2-2.5	Flat plates, luster
None	2.9	Vitreous	6.5	Often contains opaque white spots like snow flakes
None	5.0	Metallic	6-6.5	Crystal form, color
None	2.6	Vitreous to dull	7	Crystals, hardness
Pinacoidal	3.5	Vitreous	5.5-6.5	Color, with black outer coat

	CHEMICAL FORMULA	CRYSTAL SYSTEM	COLOR
Schorl (Tourmaline)	$NaFe_3^{+2}Al_6(BO_3)_3Si_6O_{18}(OH)_4$	Hexagonal (Rhombic)	Black
Siderite	$Fe^{+2}CO_3$	Hexagonal (Rhombic)	Light to dark brown
Spodumene	$LiAlSi_2O_6$	Monoclinic	Varied
Talc	$Mg_3Si_4O_{10}(OH)_2$	Monoclinic	White to greenish gray
Tremolite	$Ca_2(Mg,Fe^{+2})_5Si_8O_{22}(OH)_2$	Monoclinic	White
Wolframite	$(Fe,Mn)WO_4$	Monoclinic	Black

James W. Grandy

CLEAVAGE	SPECIFIC GRAVITY	LUSTER	HARDNESS	FAMILIARITY
None	3.1	Vitreous	7-7.5	Crystal form, striations
Rhombohedral	3.8	Vitreous to Metallic	3.5-4	Crystal form, color
Prismatic	3.1	Vitreous	6.5-7	Cleavage, striations
Basal	2.7	Pearly	1	Greasy feel, hardness
Prismatic	2.9	Silky	5-6	Needle-like structure
Pinacoidal	7.3	Sub-metallic	5-5.5	Weight—heavy

Appendix C

Official State Stones of New England

Connecticut	State Mineral	Garnet
Maine	State Mineral	Tourmaline
Massachusetts	State Gem	Rhodonite
Rhode Island	State Rock	Cumberlandite
	State Mineral	Bowenite
Vermont	State Rock	Green Stone (A metamorphic lava mixed with quartz)

Index